THE RIGHT TO VOTE

WOMEN'S RIGHT TO VOTE

by Kristine Spanier, MLIS

pogo

Ideas for Parents and Teachers

Pogo Books let children practice reading informational text while introducing them to nonfiction features such as headings, labels, sidebars, maps, and diagrams, as well as a table of contents, glossary, and index.

Carefully leveled text with a strong photo match offers early fluent readers the support they need to succeed.

Before Reading

- “Walk” through the book and point out the various nonfiction features. Ask the student what purpose each feature serves.
- Look at the glossary together. Read and discuss the words.

Read the Book

- Have the child read the book independently.
- Invite him or her to list questions that arise from reading.

After Reading

- Discuss the child’s questions. Talk about how he or she might find answers to those questions.
- Prompt the child to think more. Ask: What did you know about voting before reading this book? What more would you like to learn about it?

Pogo Books are published by Jump!
5357 Penn Avenue South
Minneapolis, MN 55419
www.jumplibrary.com

Library of Congress Cataloging-in-Publication Data

Names: Spanier, Kristine, author.
Title: Women's right to vote / by Kristine Spanier, MLIS.
Description: Minneapolis, MN: Jump!, Inc., [2025]
Series: The Right to Vote | Includes index.
Audience: Ages 7-10
Identifiers: LCCN 2023052826 (print)
LCCN 2023052827 (ebook)
ISBN 9798892131520 (hardcover)
ISBN 9798892131537 (paperback)
ISBN 9798892131544 (ebook)
Subjects: LCSH: Women–Suffrage–United States–History–Juvenile literature. | United States. Constitution. 19th Amendment–History–Juvenile literature.
Classification: LCC JK1898 .S78 2024 (print)
LCC JK1898 (ebook)
DDC 324.6/230973–dc23/eng/20240110
LC record available at https://lccn.loc.gov/2023052826
LC ebook record available at https://lccn.loc.gov/2023052827

Editor: Alyssa Sorenson
Designer: Molly Ballanger

Photo Credits: ViDI Studio/Shutterstock, cover (woman); Mega Pixel/Shutterstock, cover (sticker); YinYang/iStock, cover (sign), 4 (sign); SDI Productions/iStock, 1, 4 (people), 5; ImagePixel/Shutterstock, 3; Everett Collection/Shutterstock, 6-7; ilbusca/iStock, 8; Library of Congress/Corbis/VCG/Getty, 9; Library of Congress, 10-11, 12-13, 23; Dappled History/Alamy, 13; Bettmann/Getty, 14-15, 16-17; Shala W. Graham/Shutterstock, 18; Sourced by Piemags/PL Photography Limited/SuperStock, 19; Image Source/iStock, 20-21.

Printed in the United States of America at Corporate Graphics in North Mankato, Minnesota.

TABLE OF CONTENTS

CHAPTER 1

VOTING FOR LEADERS

In the United States, people vote for leaders. They do this during **elections**. They go to **polling places**. Or they send their votes in the mail.

To vote, U.S. **citizens** fill out **ballots**. The votes are counted. The **candidates** with the most votes win.

Help us to
win the vote

Voting is important. Why? It is how people make their voices heard. Leaders make laws that people want. Not everyone has always been able to vote. Women and people of color had to fight for this right.

WHAT DO YOU THINK?

People must be at least 18 years old to vote. Do you think younger people should be able to vote? Why or why not?

CHAPTER 2

FIGHTING FOR RIGHTS

The United States became a country in the late 1700s. Most lawmakers then were white men. They did not want women to vote. Why? They wanted women to focus on the home. Some even said women were not smart enough to vote.

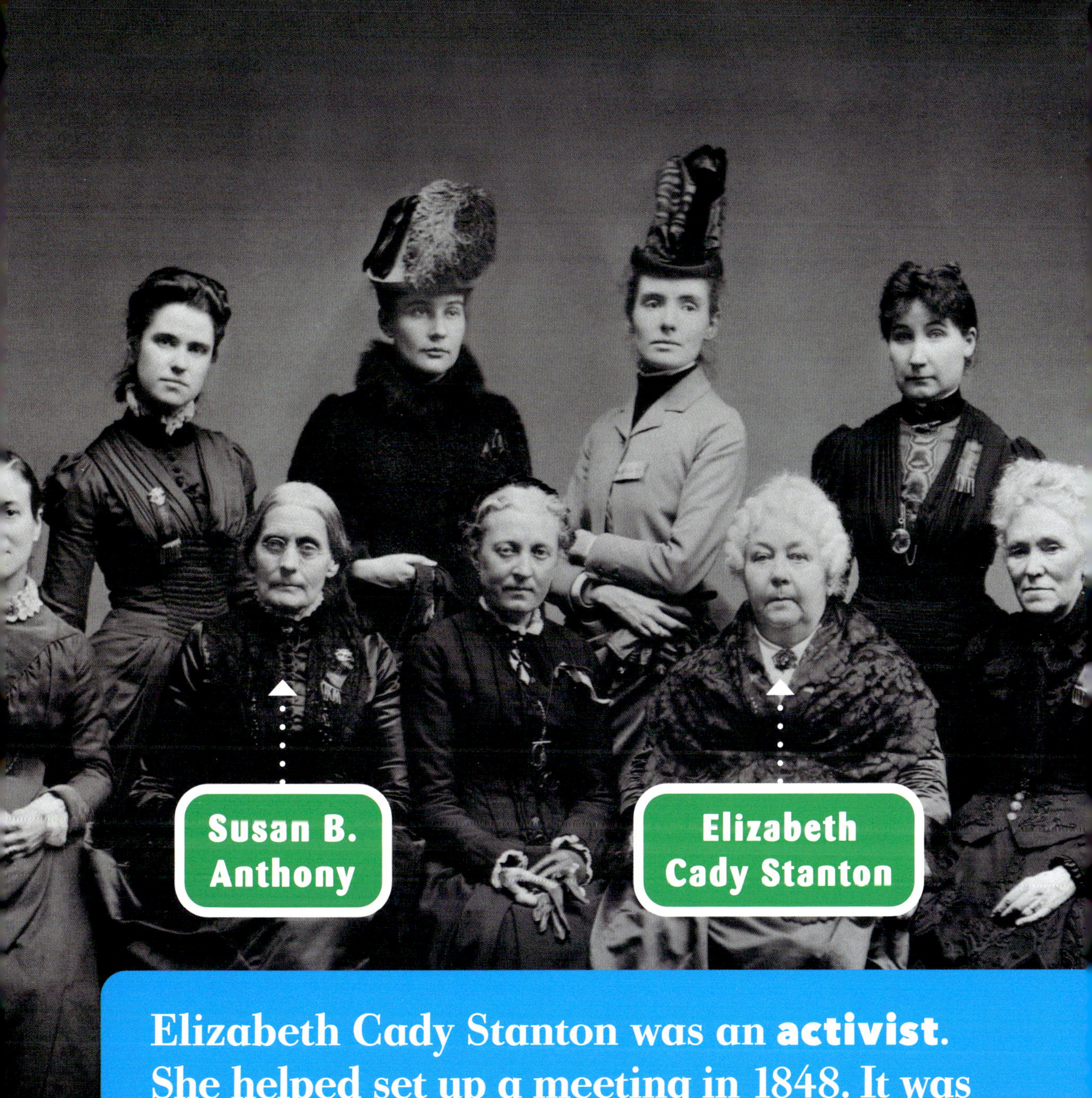

Elizabeth Cady Stanton was an **activist**. She helped set up a meeting in 1848. It was in Seneca Falls, New York. People talked at the meeting. Many agreed women should be able to vote.

In 1878, an **amendment** went to **Congress**. It was for women's **suffrage**. Congress had to pass it. Enough states had to agree. Then all women would be able to vote.

More than 30 years went by. Congress still did not pass it. People gave speeches. They signed **petitions**. In 1913, more than 5,000 people marched in Washington, D.C. This is where lawmakers work.

DID YOU KNOW?

Susan B. Anthony fought for women's rights. She voted in New York in 1872. What happened? She was arrested.

1913 march

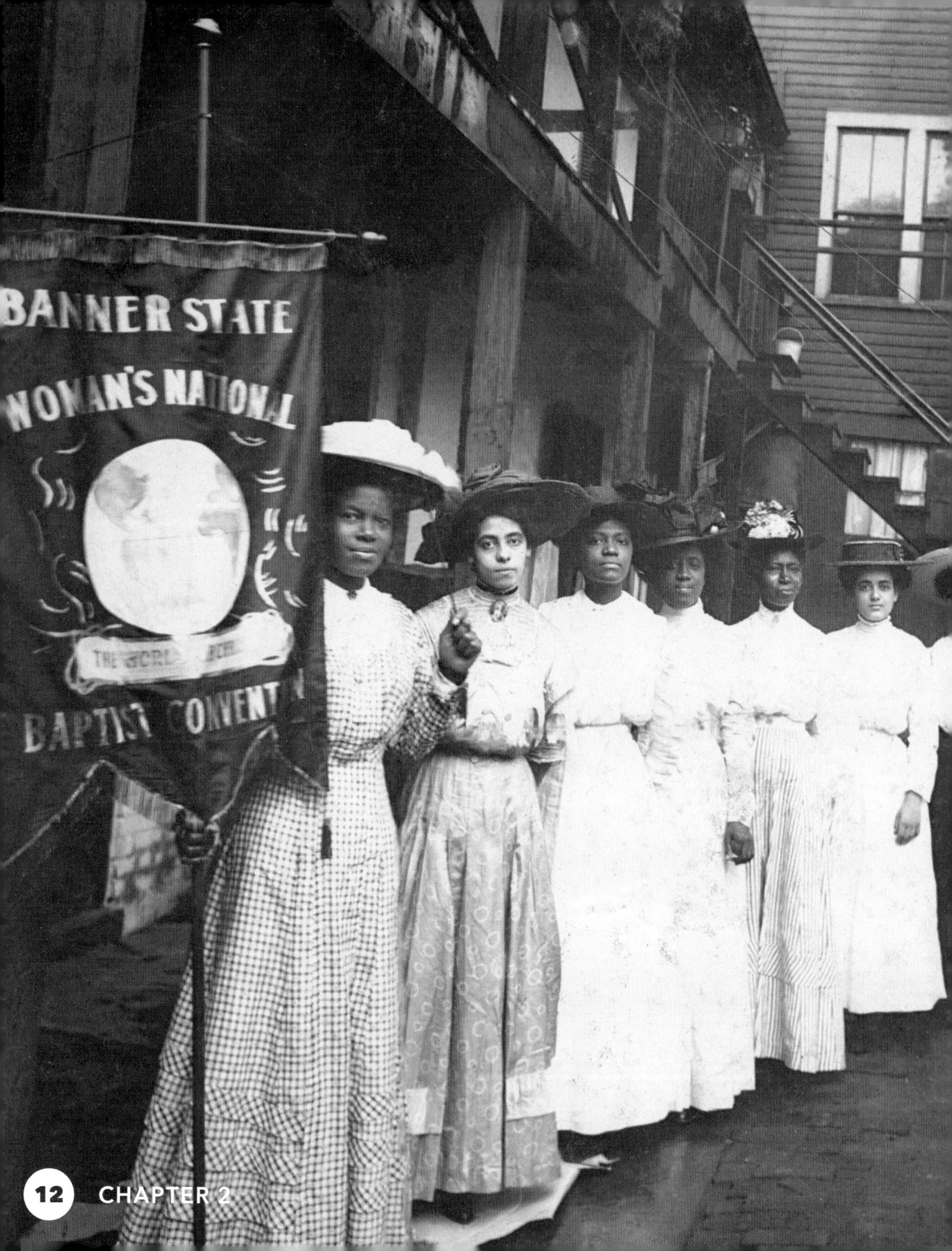
BANNER STATE
WOMAN'S NATIONAL
BAPTIST CONVENT

Many Black women fought for the right to vote. Ida B. Wells-Barnett was one. She made a group in 1913. It was for Black women. Ida knew it was important for them to vote. They could help Black people become leaders.

Ida B. Wells-Barnett

In 1918, Woodrow Wilson was president. He gave a speech. He said women should be able to vote. The next year, Congress passed the Nineteenth Amendment. It would give women this right. But 36 states had to vote yes.

DID YOU KNOW?

Before the Nineteenth Amendment, women in some parts of the country could vote. Women in Wyoming had been voting since 1870.

Woodrow Wilson

By August 18, 1920, enough states agreed. Women finally won the right to vote! They celebrated.

Women of color still struggled. Some states passed laws. They tried to stop people of color from voting. In 1965, Congress put an end to this.

TAKE A LOOK!

When did the first 36 states vote for the Nineteenth Amendment? Take a look!

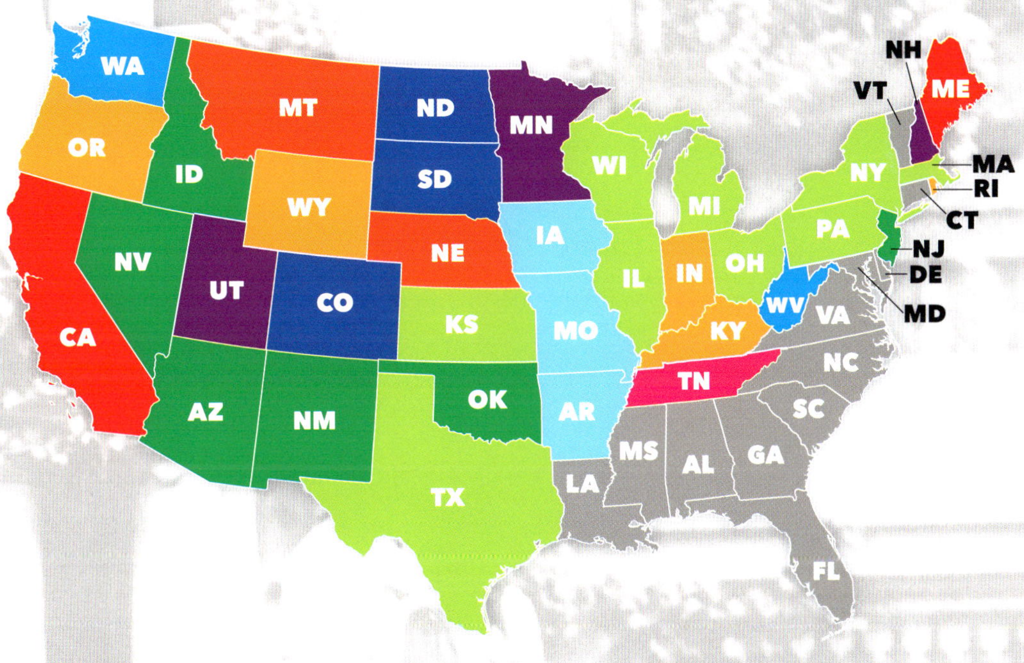

June 1919
July 1919
August 1919
September 1919
November 1919
December 1919
January 1920
February 1920
March 1920
August 1920
States that voted for the Nineteenth Amendment after it passed

CHAPTER 3

WOMEN'S RIGHTS TODAY

Women still fight for equal rights. They can vote. But many do not get the same jobs as men. Women are often paid less. They work for change. How? They **protest**. They make their voices heard.

In 2021, Kamala Harris made history. How? She became the first female vice president.
Kamala Harris
VICE PRESIDENT OF THE UNITED STATES

FOR
BALLOTS
SMITH
for
PRESIDENT

As of 2023, the United States had not yet had a female president. But women have held every other political office. Women who vote help make this happen! When do you think the first female president will be elected? Maybe it will be you!

WHAT DO YOU THINK?

Do you think it is important to let all U.S. citizens vote? Why or why not?

QUICK FACTS & TOOLS

TIMELINE

Women spent many years fighting for the right to vote. Take a look.

JULY 19–20, 1848
The Seneca Falls Convention takes place. This is the first women's rights gathering in the United States.

1878
An amendment to give women the right to vote is brought to Congress. Congress does not pass it.

MARCH 3, 1913
More than 5,000 people march for women's suffrage in Washington, D.C.

1917
Women meet outside the White House. They want President Wilson to support women's suffrage. Some are arrested.

JUNE 4, 1919
Congress passes the Nineteenth Amendment.

AUGUST 18, 1920
Enough states agree to the amendment. Women win the right to vote!

1965
Congress passes the Voting Rights Act. This says states cannot stop people of color from voting.

2021
Kamala Harris becomes the first female vice president of the United States.

GLOSSARY

activist: A person who supports a cause and believes in taking action to change things.

amendment: A change made to a law or legal document.

ballots: Pieces of paper that people use to mark which political candidates they want to hold office.

candidates: People who run for office in an election.

citizens: People who belong to a country and have full rights.

Congress: The branch of the U.S. government that makes laws.

elections: The acts or processes of deciding something by voting.

petitions: Letters signed by many people asking leaders to change their policies or actions.

polling places: Buildings or locations at which people vote.

protest: To demonstrate against something.

suffrage: The right to vote.

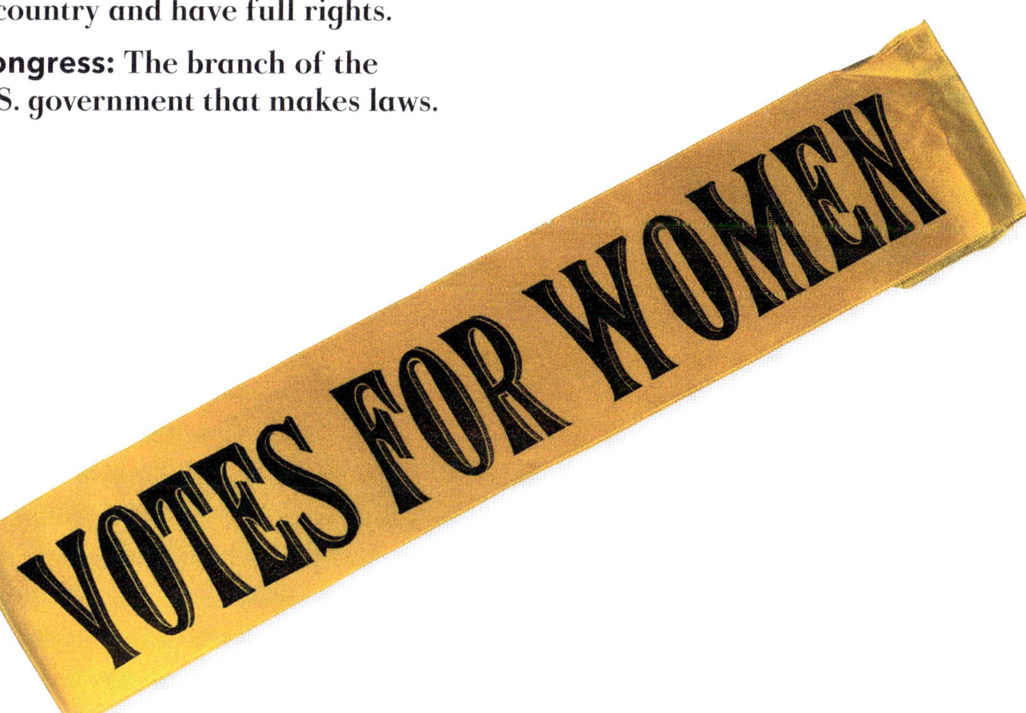

INDEX

TO LEARN MORE

Finding more information is as easy as 1, 2, 3.

1. Go to www.factsurfer.com
2. Enter "women'srighttovote" into the search box.
3. Choose your book to see a list of websites.